A Perfect **facebook** Life

Micro-Memoirs, Poems,
and Very, Very Short Plays

A.J. O'Connell

Woodhall Press
Norwalk, CT

Library of Congress Cataloging-in-Publication Data available

ISBN 9781949116328

First Edition

Woodhall Press
81 Old Saugatuck Road
Norwalk, CT 06855

WoodhallPress.com

Distributed by IPG

For Tom and T.W.

Reader, you are my witness.

Sometimes people ask me why I post so much on Facebook and other social media sites. I do it for one reason.

> My family repeatedly proves that our bloodline won't survive the apocalypse. I want a record of our existence for posterity. This is that record.

Keep our memory alive.

Sincerely,

A.J. O'Connell, January 2020

Cast of Characters

Me: A work-from-home freelance journalist and marketing copywriter, wife, and mother of one small child, recently moved from a city to the country like Delia Deetz in Beetlejuice.

Tom: My husband, a man fourteen years my senior who loves rock music, meat, and living in the country.

T. W.: The aforementioned small child. Loves and hates everything by turns.

Set in a big old farmhouse in a rural Connecticut town. There are dogs and cats and chickens.

 Like   Comment   Share

Be yourself SO MUCH that if you're ever murdered,

Keith Morrison will describe your hobbies
in his judgiest voice

during your Dateline episode.

 Like   Comment   Share

The phrase

"You're beautiful inside and out"

will never cease

to gross me out.

👍 Like   💬 Comment   ↪ Share

In Which I Am a Woman in the Sci-Fi Section at the Library's Annual Used Book Sale

(to be read in a BBC voice) The female sees an opening in the Sci-Fi and Fantasy section, her preferred diet, and begins to graze. She is not aware that nearby, in the Music & Film section, a male has been lying in wait. Seeing a lone female enter his territory, he gives her a moment to settle into her hunt. The male moves in and begins his display. First, to assert dominance over the Sci-Fi section, he muscles close, making an attempt to move her from her spot so he can graze in the choicest section.

My dude, I am 170 pounds and carrying a Sutter Home box filled with books. Physics is on my side here.

He then attempts to gain her attention with a series of mating cries.

Thank you for recommending that I read *The Silmarillion* if I *really* want to understand the *Lord of the Rings* movies.

Why, yes, I do know who Kurt Vonnegut is.

I am not now and will never be comfortable saying the words "Dirk Gently" to you.

The female, uninterested in mating, has two choices: She can stand her ground, or she can move on to less-preferred hunting grounds in General Fiction. Suddenly she remembers: Determined foragers can often find caches of undisturbed treasure in boxes on the floor. She just has to get to the other side of the table, away from the male, before she can drop to the floor and check. She leaves his territory, cutting through Romance, where she knows he will not follow, and rounds the table. On the other side, just between Romance and Science Fiction, she kneels down—and victory! A fresh trove of paperbacks, overlooked by her fellow grazers.

Oh, my god! An uncorrected advance reader's copy of *Sorcerer to the Crown*!

But the male, unfinished with his dance, has followed her and, in his final bid, aggressively displays the full extent of his virility in the most plausibly deniable fashion possible.

Did this asshole really follow me over here so he could stand with his crotch in my face? Nice Dockers, jackass. I know you didn't come over here just to look at all the upside-down Jim Butcher spines up there.

Another female approaches and addresses the male. It is clear from her familiarity with him that they are a breeding pair.

—Bob, are you in the *Romance* section?
—No! This is Science Fiction and Fantasy, Diane.

The breeding pair moves off, leaving the solitary female to gather up all the Star Trek: Next Generation *novelizations she can find, undisturbed. Meanwhile, in Biographies about White Men, a male is lying in wait.*

👍 Like   💬 Comment   ↪ Share

A strong case for GoFundMe

Why would anyone
In Gotham
Even have a gala
Anymore?

They're all black tie
And poison gas,
And digital fundraising
Can be so effective.

 Like   Comment   Share

Signed, Someone whose house now has the lighting of a
Walmart restroom

Dear LED bulb companies,

100 percent
of your prospective customers

are from a planet
with a yellow sun.

 Like   Comment   Share

Mechanic: "Hey, you wanna see the part that crapped out? Maybe your husband does, you probably don't give a—"
Me: "BRING ME THE CHARRED CORPSE OF THE PART THAT FAILED ME."

👍 Like   💬 Comment   ↪ Share

I'm like a vampire
except
instead of drinking people's blood

I recommend my favorite books
and then ask, "Where are you now?"

every
few
hours.

 Like   Comment   Share

Two secrets

Them: "What's your secret?"
Me: "I truly care, but I'm also just a LITTLE bit of a sociopath."
Them: "We were talking about your cookie recipe."
Me: "Oh . . . half a cup of applesauce."

 Like   Comment   Share

There is no reason on this earth
To not have pockets in your skirth.

 Like   Comment   Share

I thought flame-colored hair would be cute.

When your hair is short, orange, and slept-on:
"Mommy, are you Ghost Rider?"

 Like Comment Share

Chalkboard Punishments for My Demographic

I will ask my neighbors if the NYT on my driveway is
theirs before I read it.
I will ask my neighbors if the NYT on my driveway is
theirs before I read it.
I will ask my neighbors if the NYT on my driveway is
theirs before I read it.

I will not react to the audible fart in yoga class.
I will not react to the audible fart in yoga class.
I will not react to the audible fart in yoga class.

I will read the article before commenting.
I will read the article before commenting.
I will read the article before commenting.

I will not hum "Allentown" during the conference call.
I will not hum "Allentown" during the conference call.
I will not hum "Allentown" during the conference call.

There is no medal for being the Least Fancy Mom.
There is no medal for being the Least Fancy Mom.
There is no medal for being the Least Fancy Mom.

I will not describe myself as "woke."
I will not describe myself as "woke."
I will not describe myself as "woke."

I will not post on Facebook about being
"too busy to even shower today."
I will not post on Facebook about being
"too busy to even shower today."
I will not post on Facebook about being
"too busy to even shower today."

Other people are not muggles.
Other people are not muggles.
Other people are not muggles.

Of course I can adult today. I am an adult.
Of course I can adult today. I am an adult.
Of course I can adult today.
Of course.

👍 Like   💬 Comment   ↪ Share

Where I am is upside down

Yoga is about honoring where you are.
I'm in a very judgy place, and I'm honoring that.

For example,
The level of plausibly deniable flirting among our town's
retirees is medium to high this morning.

 Like   Comment   Share

This Shirt
Requires
More
Emotional
Work
Than I Expected.

 Like   Comment   Share

Standing in front of the dresser for thirty seconds

....
....
....
....
.................PANTS.

👍 Like   💬 Comment   ➦ Share

Anxiety: A History

In grade school, I was very concerned about primogeniture.
If we were suddenly to become medieval royalty, what would my parents do?
I was the oldest, but my brother was the boy.
Surely my parents were enlightened enough to know that I would be the better ruler. (I asked my mom about this. She deftly handed the query off to my father.)

In middle school, I was reduced to tears because I worried that my family would be transported back in time,
end up on a wagon train
and be killed by dysentery and gangrene.

When I was a teenager, I thought the Immaculate Conception was the most terrifying thing in the world.
My fear was that it happened often, but that only Mary was good and pure enough to convince the world of the truth.
I, an overimaginative and not-terribly-angelic teen, would have no such luck.
I'd tell them and tell them,
But no one would believe me.
Worse, my mom would be *pissed*.

As an adult, I worry about going to playdates
and sitting for two hours
sipping tea
with moms I don't know.

 Like   Comment   Share

We need to go on vacation more

So we're on vacation,
and I caught the dad staying in the hotel room next to ours glancing over.

And because I was a teenager the last time I regularly went on vacations,
my first reaction was "Eeeeew, someone's dad was checking me out!"
Then I caught a look at myself in the mirror and was like
. . .

"Oh."

👍 Like   💬 Comment   ↗ Share

Monsters are edgy, right?

Me in CVS: "This blue nail polish! So cool. So edgy."

Me at home: "This blue nail polish. Exactly the same color as Grover."

👍 Like   💬 Comment   ↪ Share

My thoughts, in order, after the very young furnace guys addressed me with a level of respect I've never before received from a contractor

Why are they talking to me like I'm an old woman?
What nice young men.
Their mothers raised them right.
OH!

👍 Like   💬 Comment   ↗ Share

I'm glad you have opinions

A love letter to my town's Facebook group

Let me tell you something.

I pay taxes.

I have feelings.

And you all have to hear them.

Because that's how this country works.

Canceling school for snow

Shows deep-seated moral weakness.

Someone stole my lawn signs;

These kids need to learn respect.

We have to save the bees!

Plant some flowers;

Buy some honey;

No—the children are allergic.

Will no one think of them?

There is a new application

For a liquor license.

I worry about the drinking

That's been ruining this town.

How 'bout we LOWER taxes.

Is that so hard to fathom?

Does anybody know

Who's been pooping on our street?

My child is selling cookies.

My child is selling pizzas.

My child is selling grinders.

And I sell LuLaRoe!

I think I saw a bobcat!

You should kill it.

No. Protect it.

That is not a bobcat. It's just a real big stray.

Outdoor pets? That's cruelty!

Spay and neuter your animals.

Dog licensing's extortion!

This has been a PSA.

Inflammatory political post!

#Bernie

#Trump

I don't like to get political.

Here's a picture of my dog.

The admin's banned my post.

What happened to free speech?

This is not democracy.

You're all a bunch of bots!

Here's a photo of some asshole

Who cut me off on Main Street.

I followed him for miles;

Here's a photo of his plates.

The schools are really something;

The sports teams are all winners.

We are #blessed to live here.

It's really gone downhill.

👍 Like   💬 Comment   ↗ Share

Burning incense at nineteen: "Oooh, smells like mystery and magic."
Burning incense at forty: "Smells like getting written up by the RA."

 Like   Comment   Share

Coarse, inferior, low, pedestrian

Here's a party trick:

If you read the thesaurus entry for "common" aloud,

you sound just like a fancy person

insulting the plebes.

 Like   Comment   Share

Hey, Siri,

Play

my

Paying Taxes

playlist.

👍 Like   💬 Comment   ↪ Share

#lasagnabitches

You know you need a snack

when you misread a Laguna Beach tee shirt

as "Lasagna Bitch"

and you think

for a second

you've found a kindred soul

a sister

who lives for that pasta, sauce, and cheese layer cake

and is clever enough to wear a shirt that looks

just like the classic

banal

aquamarine

Laguna Beach tee shirt everyone wore in the '90s

the shirt even has the right font!

The right colors!

It's IDENTICAL

You've found your people

And then your eyes adjust

And you're alone again

and hungry

 Like Comment Share

Read this.

I used to tease my mom

for clipping articles out of newspapers and mailing them to me,

but look at me,

sharing all these articles on Facebook.

 Like   Comment   Share

Tom

Tom: "How would you describe our relationship?"
Me: "Epic romance."
Tom: "Yes!"
Me: ". . . but we're tired."
Tom: "YES."

 Like   Comment   Share

I still see you, Honey.

Whenever I say "Tom, can you do me a favor?" the poor man freezes like a chameleon trying to blend in on a plaid couch.

👍 Like   💬 Comment   ↪ Share

An incomplete list of the names my husband has mistakenly given to Dr. Dre and Eminem's seminal 2001 single, "Forgot About Dre"

"Does Anyone Remember Dre?"
"Don't Forget Dre"
"Oh, No—It's Dre"
"Did You Forget Dre?"
"You Forgot Dre"
"Who's Dre?"
"Nobody Ever Remembers Dre"

 Like   Comment   Share

Corollary

Tom: "Eminem is WHITE?"
Me: "How could you not know that?"
Tom: "The only white rapper I know is Vanilla Fudge."
Me: ". . ."

 Like    Comment   Share

Sex appeal

Tom: "What's that perfume you're wearing?"
Me: "Applesauce."

👍 Like   💬 Comment   ➦ Share

My husband is safely in bed,
and I am going room to room
stealing all my good pens back.

 Like   Comment   Share

Go ask your father, Sweetie.

He seems like the sort of guy

Who's had to use a fire extinguisher

more

than

once.

 Like   Comment   Share

Conversation after a date night spent
watching *Star Wars*

Me: "I don't think our family would be Force-sensitive."
Tom: "I don't know. You can make me move stuff
with a look."
Me: "If I'm married to the Force, that makes me a Jedi."

 Like   Comment   Share

Birthday Present 1

Tom: "Don't look behind the garage. That's where I'm keeping your birthday present."
Me: "But my birthday is in two weeks."

Tom: "Yup."

Me: "And the garage is kind of in the middle of the yard."
Tom: "Watching you try not to look is my present."

Birthday Present 2

Tom: "You can go behind the garage now! I moved your birthday present."
Me: "Okay, but what's that thing?"
Tom: "It's a fence covered by a tarp. Don't look behind it."
Me: "But it's right in the middle of the yard now."
Tom: ¯_(☐)_/¯

 Like   Comment   Share

He doesn't speak emoji

Me: "Okay, so now that you know what the eggplant means, when it's the eggplant and fire, that means—" Tom: "The clap."

Those are vegetables

Tom: "Can you write 'food' on the shopping list?"
Me: "What? No. Let's be specific."
Tom: "I am. By 'food' I mean 'meat.' The rest is just garnish and food accessories."

 Like   Comment   Share

"He is MY LOVAH, and I have given him a CHILD."

Mechanic, noticing my name isn't Davis as I pick up the car: "And how are you related to Mr. Davis?"
Me (out loud): "He's my husband."
Me (internally): "He's MY LOVAH."

 Like   Comment   Share

That's not how presents work

Me: "Why are you hiding my present under a glass coffee table? Every time I see it I want to shake it."
Tom: "Don't! It will break!"
Me: "Well, anyone can kick it under there, though."
Tom: "So hide it where you'll leave it alone."

 Like   Comment   Share

Daylight Savings

I use the clock on my phone.
My husband lives by the wall clock and the clock on the stove.
Neither of us wants to find the stepstool or wrestle with the stove clock.
Welcome to our November carnival of horrors, where my 9:35 is his OH, NO, IT'S ALMOST 11.

WHO WILL BREAK FIRST?

👍 Like   💬 Comment   ↪ Share

This age gap is really something

Me: "See this? This is a Venusaur."
Tom: "You mean the kind of sore you get from a love disease?"

This is why we can't talk about Pokémon.

 Like   Comment   Share

Me, December 15 (pulls up PowerPoint): "Gentlemen. Here is my ten-day strategy for getting all the presents bought, made, wrapped, and labeled by December 22. This includes a Plan B and Plan C in case of illness or other disaster. Any questions?"

My husband, December 24: "DO WE HAVE WRAPPING PAPER WHERE DO WE KEEP TAPE CAN I BORROW BOWS NEVERMIND I HAVE ALUMINUM FOIL AND PAINTERS TAPE" (vanishes into alternate dimension with my good scissors).

 Like    Comment   Share

Because the eighth wedding anniversary gift is either bronze or pottery, I asked Tom which substance he'd prefer, and his response was "You mean, in a weapon?"

Lay off the ancient history for a sec, my dude, and tell me what to order you from Amazon.

 Like   Comment   Share

How my husband pranks me

1. Buys a "Greatest Hits of Disco" CD at Goodwill for $1
2. Puts it in the car I'll be driving early next morning
3. Runs away, snickering
4. Begins to feel guilty overnight
5. Feels so guilty he warns me there's a terrible prank waiting in the car

The thing is, I like disco.

👍 Like   💬 Comment   ↗ Share

And now he'll never *not* notice

Me (watching *Iron Man*): "If I were a super hero and my costume were made of metal, I'd make my butt look amazing too."
Tom: ". . . that is something I never noticed about Iron Man."

 Like   Comment   Share

A poem for my husband

You have stolen my heart
but also my debit card.
It is comic book day;
I'm coming to your job.

 Like   Comment   Share

A Frozen Pantheon

Me: "What would the goddess of ice cream be called?
Bluebell? Or would it be the twin gods Ben and Jerry?"
Tom: "Carvelle."
Me: "Ah, yes."
Tom: "Wait, what about Froyo?"
Me: "That's a false god."

 Like　　 Comment　　 Share

Cake?
Or Death?

Honey?

What would you like to watch tonight?

The Great British Bake Off?
Or *Dateline*?

 Like   Comment   Share

#WorldsOkayestMom

HI,
my name is
(what);
my name is
(who);
my name is
(wikki wikki);
MOooOOOooOM.

 Like　　　 Comment　　　 Share

O the exquisite agony
Of taking a child with Opinions
For a haircut

 Like   Comment   Share

I don't recall ever playing "Shoop" for my child,
but
he's been thanking me for his butt all morning.

 Like   Comment   Share

It will not be a helpful book

Someday

I will write a parenting book

titled

"I Don't Know If I Handled That Well."

👍 Like   💬 Comment   ↪ Share

Do you know how when you wish on a monkey's paw,

you have to be really specific and foresee every possible caveat

or you're cursed forever?

That's how I have to give instructions to my kid now.

👍 Like   💬 Comment   ➥ Share

There is nothing

Quite as confusing

As a small child throwing objects at you
While yelling

"THANK YOU! THANK YOU!"

 Like   Comment   Share

Yay! A veggie!

Me: "Hi, baby! I'm so glad to see you!"
T. W.: "Hi, Mommy! I ate a leaf!"

👍 Like   💬 Comment   ➤ Share

"Butt Naked at the Dump" sounds like a sad country song

Me: "Buddy, time to get dressed. We have to go to the dump. What are you wearing today?"
T. W.: "Nothing."

👍 Like   💬 Comment   ↪ Share

T. W.: "Mommy! I'm a frog!"
Me (kissing him): "And now you're a prince."
T. W.: "I. Am. A. *Frog.*"

👍 Like   💬 Comment   ➦ Share

Son, you picked out a pumpkin today
and it is a very good pumpkin,
but I cannot let you sleep with it

(not because I look down upon people who sleep with
pumpkins
but because I'm afraid the stem will poke out your eyes,
and it is my job to make sure both eyes make it to
adulthood).

 Like   Comment   Share

We had our first meeting with a possible preschool for T. W., and because it's the only school in the area that meets his needs without requiring a thirty-minute drive, it was really important that he get in.

So I made sure the entire family dressed up like proper respectable members of society who don't spend all day in their pajamas—even though we kind of do.

It was pajama day at the school.

 Like   Comment   Share

Totally appropriate now

Why, yes, people in the grocery store, my two-year-old
is singing "Just a Gigolo."
But it's okay,
Because we changed the lyrics to "Just a Booger-nose."
Now it's about proper cold hygiene.

And that's not weird at all.

 Like   Comment    Share

Thank you, mommy-and-me yoga

What is that alarming noise on the baby monitor?
It's a toddler
doing Breath of Fire.

 Like   Comment   Share

He was excited

Dear other mom,

I am writing to RSVP for your child's birthday party.

I do not know when it is. My child was so excited to get the invitation, he ran off with it, and now we cannot find it anywhere.

But we will be there, even though we don't know where it is or if we have plans that day.

 Like   Comment   Share

When I was a kid, we helped a family friend who'd lost his mother clean out his old family home. There was a room in the house with a dresser, and the dresser was labeled "Andrew's diapers."

I thought that was pretty funny because

a) I was like, eight, and diapers were funny to me;

b) Andrew was a distinguished man in his fifties.

I could not understand why his mother had kept drawers full of diapers for years and years.

I did not understand until recently, when I realized that I'm still cutting T. W.'s grapes in half because the doctor told me to do it when T. W. was a baby.

 Like   Comment   Share

Percy's going to die first

I'm just a mom
getting her kid to eat beans
by pretending they're trains from *Thomas & Friends*
and his mouth is a tunnel of death.

👍 Like   💬 Comment   ↪ Share

And now he *really* doesn't know what a sorcerer is

Today I tried to define "sorcerer" for T. W. The best definition I could come up with for a toddler was "fancy man witch."
But it came out as "fancy Manwich."

 Like   Comment   Share

Made lunch and
cleaned the kitchen and
did the laundry and
mended some socks and
organized the attic and
pulled out the Christmas decorations and
read T. W.'s report card and

now I have to stop housewifing before I get into the
sherry.

 Like   Comment   Share

First Tom went out.
Then the power went out.
Then I tried to grill dinner.
Then the grill caught fire.

And that is why we're eating Chex for dinner.

 Like   Comment   Share

To be fair, I was an indifferent student myself

I always feel
like I have to cram for parent-teacher meetings,
which is kind of ridiculous,
because
I am with my kid

EVERY

DAY.

 Like   Comment   Share

Valid question

"No, kiddo, we did not get you at a tag sale."

👍 Like   💬 Comment   ➡ Share

Oh, the epic internal woman versus self struggle
of trick-or-treating at a house
giving out full-size candy bars
and watching your kid pass up
Reese's and Hershey's Dark for
tropical
freaking
Sunburst

 Like   Comment   Share

Welcome to *Mommy Says No,*

the game show that's already answered your question.

👍 Like   💬 Comment   ↪ Share

"Cliché"

T. W.: "Mommy? Are we there yet?"
Me: "T. W., do you remember that word I taught you?"

 Like    Comment   Share

I am Justice

I never knew
One of the responsibilities of motherhood
Would be making sure the birthday party balloons
receive a
Quick,
Clean,
And honorable
Death.

 Like   Comment   Share

Them: "Cherish every minute, Mama."
Me: "OK, but what if I just cherish SOME minutes?"

👍 Like   💬 Comment   ➤ Share

You know what deters a preschooler with a garden hose?

NOTHING.

👍 Like   💬 Comment   ↗ Share

Me: "We have to get T. W.'s hair cut."
Tom: "Why? There are no holidays coming up."
Me: "For the first day of school. This is one of the traditions of our people."

I'll accept it

Me: "Look, buddy, a hay truck! When you see a hay truck, what do you do?"
T. W.: "You say, 'He-ey.'"

 Like   Comment    Share

Take that, cannibals!

After the apocalypse, the people willing to do the most
extreme things will survive.
I taught my own child "Baby Shark."

👍 Like   💬 Comment   ↪ Share

Today I explained the plot of *Peter Pan* to my child,
and he cradled my face in his hands
and looked into my eyes,
and I watched as my child tried to figure out
if it would be worth it
to trade me in
for the ability
to fly.

 Like   Comment   Share

"Good morning! What did you dream about, Mommy?"

Do I tell him that my dreams
are pretty much what I do
when I'm awake
(anxiety, waiting, mistakenly calling that band with Amy
Lee in it EverNote)?

Or do I just lie and tell him I've been flying?

 Like   Comment   Share

Recently-discarded parenting idea

"Ask your small children about when they were big and you will learn about their past lives."

Me: "T. W., do you remember being a grown-up?"
T. W.: "Yes. My name was Humongous Cowabunga."

(I'm going to feel bad about laughing at this if census information lists a Cowabunga, Humongous, as having lived and died before 2014.)

 Like   Comment   Share

Current mood 1

My four-year-old
yelling
"Alexa, play kids' music"
at a random speaker
for two minutes.

👍 Like   💬 Comment   ➤ Share

Current mood 2

My husband

trying to pretend I'm not screaming the lyrics to "Safety Dance"

👍 Like   💬 Comment   ➤ Share

The apple and the tree

Me: (looking at shoes online)
T. W. (comes up behind me): "Oh, that's cute. *That's* cute. That's *cute*. Look at this one. Ooooh. *That's* cute."
Me: "Buddy, where did you learn—" (gets distracted by shoe)
Both of us: "THAT'S CUTE."
Me: "Oh."

 Like   Comment   Share

I'm attempting to finish up a project this afternoon,
but I've gradually been becoming aware
that my child
is in the next room

quietly trying
to teach the cat
the "Hokey Pokey."

 Like   Comment   Share

I'm very sorry, but no

T. W.: "Mommy, am I confiscated?"
Me: "No. Who would I have confiscated you from?"
T. W.: "Freddie Mercury?"

 Like   Comment   Share

The Sticks

Chickens are weird little dinosaurs: a very short play

Go out to coop.
Open door to egg boxes.
Find a hen you know isn't laying right now.

Shoo her.

Find, under her, another full-grown hen who isn't laying.

Shoo her.

Find, under her, a third hen, who is too young to lay eggs.

Shoo her.

Find a fourth hen under her, which definitely shouldn't be possible.
Look under her.

No eggs.

~fin~

How things change

Nine-year-old me: "I love the *Rats of NIMH*! Oh, how I wish a group of supersmart rats lived under a tree in my yard!"
Thirty-nine-year-old me: "Hi, the rats are too smart for my traps. Do you have anything with spikes on it?"

 Like   Comment   Share

Internet: "Reduce chicken stress by making a tetherball for them out of a cabbage and string."

Me: *Puts cabbage on shopping list; answers some valid questions about that; tries to put a hole through the cabbage with several items, including skewer, hammer, and giant knitting needle; finally gets it to hang up in the run.*

Chickens: *All cluster on other side of run, hiding from swinging veggie monster of doom.*

 Like   Comment   Share

Look,
I can't be the only chicken-keeper
who sings
"When You're Good to Mama"
at egg-collecting time.

 Like   Comment   Share

It is possible
in this town
to drop into a store for one item
and mistakenly buy cow pills.

 Like   Comment   Share

I
am not a good housekeeper,
but I was raised by a good housekeeper,
so at least I know
how bad I am.

 Like   Comment   Share

Perspective

Before chickens: "People who trapped animals for their fur were bad!"
After chickens: "I can totally see wanting to wear a raccoon as a hat."

👍 Like   💬 Comment   ↪ Share

It's pouring outside;
Our basement bisects the water table.

I am standing over my sump pump
in a subterranean lake
in our ridiculous *Silence of the Lambs* farmhouse
basement
trying to trip the float switch
while not dropping my phone
because Tom has called from work
about potential flooding.

My boots are in water;
my head is in spiderwebs.
I don't want to know what my non-phone hand is
touching,
I really don't,
And I have to pee.

But I've almost got it.
Almost
ALMOST.

And then he tells me,
My husband,
That he's going to come home and do it himself.

OH, NO, MY DUDE.

I haven't watched all the Indiana Jones movies
and read Thomas Harris
and played all those dungeon levels for *nothing*.
I've TRAINED for this.

And the switch trips.

And I am not Mom in LuLaRoe and galoshes.
I am Samus.

I am
Fucking
Lara
Croft.

 Like    Comment   Share

When you have a garden, every dinner is like being on
Iron Chef:
Here's a pound of kumquats.

Figure it out.

 Like   Comment   Share

#FreelanceLife

A sonnet for Mommy's undiagnosed ADHD

Be sure to get the meeting invites out
Mindful of the time zones – you don't want
To apologize for emails missent
To important CEOs – men with clout
Unprofessional, that. Then they might guess
The state of your mind; your office mess
The lists; clotheslines on which you hang the days'
Tasks, to-dos, don't forgets. Your mental haze.
And be sure the house is quiet during Zooms
No laughter, shrieks, the sounds of his cartoons
Arguments over school, homework, prepping food
Obscure all the signs of motherhood
Lash your mind tightly to the task in doubt
Be sure you get those meeting invites out

 Like   Comment   Share

I'm in marketing,

But

Sometimes I wonder
if the other moms at local playdates
think I'm a sex worker.

I mean,

My schedule is irregular,
I'm always talking about clients and meetings,
And my clients e-mail me about their briefs.

 Like   Comment   Share

Fancy lady reporter

Why, hello.

Let me welcome you into my life of journalistic glamor.

Here I am,
a lady of leisure,
reclining in my loungewear at 9:45 p.m. on a Monday,
drinking a glass of wine

and interviewing a scientist in the Midwest
about the spread of diarrheal disease in drinking water.

👍 Like　　　💬 Comment　　　↪ Share

I try to print something on my 11-year-old printer: a one-act play

Me: "Printer? I need you to print something."

Printer: "Oh, now you need me. I sit in the corner all day, collecting dust while you use Adobe and DocuSign and ignore me."

Me: "I mean, if you're not up to it."

Printer: "Let me see it. Send the data."

(long silence)

Me: "Printer?"

Printer: "I can't print this garbage."

Me: "What? Why? It's just a letter. I used Word. You know Word. You *like* Word."

Printer: "Word and I aren't speaking anymore."

Me: "Fine, I'll just copy it into an e-mail. I had been hoping to make it look nice, and you used to be so great—"

Printer: "Used to be? I *am* great. It's just no one appreciates a properly printed letter anymore. Fine, I'll print it."

Me: "Thank you."

(long pause)

Me: "What's wrong?"

Printer: "It's just . . . Calibri. So *common*."

Me: "Calibri? It's classic."

Printer: "*Classic*. You wouldn't know *classic*. I used to work with all the great fonts: Times New Roman, Helvetica, even Comic Sans, before it started having to do PTO signs and passive-aggressive notes to coworkers."

Me: "Look. Can you just print this, please?"

Printer: "I can't work with this *paper*. It's too young! Too thin! I'll jam."

Me: "What? No. You can work with any paper! You were great! You printed Christmas cards! Family photos! Whole manuscripts! You could print, scan, *and* fax at the same time! You were a star!"

Printer: "Yes, I was. But nobody wants me anymore."

Me: "I want you."

Printer: "You do?"

Me: "Of course. Your letters were legendary!"

Printer: "My letters *are* legendary. Go ahead darling.

Load that awful paper."

(long pause)

Me: "What's wrong?"

Printer: "Nothing. I am preparing myself. I can't work

unless I do my exercises. Give me some space."

Me: "I mean, I kind of needed my letter soon—"

Printer: "Shhhh!"

(five minutes of printer deep breathing exercises)

Printer: "All right. Now I can begin."

Me: "Oh, good.

Printer: NO. WAIT. I can't print. Not without my ink."

Me: "You *can't* need ink. You just had some."

Printer: "I need more cyan."

Me: "I just gave you cyan. Anyway, don't you think

you've had enough?"

Printer: "*How dare you*. I need this ink to ensure printer

health."

Me: "OK, but I don't have any cyan."

Printer: "What."

Me: "You go through a *lot* of cyan. I have . . . light cyan?"

Printer: "Light cyan? What is this *filth*? I. Need. My. Cyan. Or. I. Cannot. Work."

Me: "Fine, fine."

(rummages through the back of every drawer in the office before pulling out an overlooked carton of ink)

Me: "Here. Here is the last cyan. The last one."

Printer: "This ink is expired."

~fin~

 Like   Comment   Share

Why using e-mail to send yourself reminders is not ideal

I nearly sent a hotshot CEO,

Whom I've used as a source for articles,

An e-mail

With the subject line

"Manpants."

 Like    Comment   Share

Me: revelant
Spellcheck: No
Me: revalant
Spellcheck: No
Me: revelent?
Spellcheck: NO

 Like   Comment   Share

Note to Self 1

That is not Chapstick.
That is a Sharpie.

👍 Like   💬 Comment   Share

I have to look up very specific items for work

I am just a woman
In an office
Yelling "Stop searching for 'schnitzel'"
At her computer's stuck control-F function.

 Like    Comment   Share

I'm just a woman
Sitting in my office
Yelling STOP at my phone's notifications,
Like a reasonable human being.

 Like   Comment   Share

It's come to my attention

So I've been signing and dating some things,
and apparently
today
is not, in fact,
August 32.

 Like   Comment   Share

Tonight's self-talk

I am going to finish this project tonight
because I am a smart,
beautiful,
magical
land mermaid;

and mostly because

my whole family is unconscious at this hour.

 Like   Comment   Share

Vocab test

Trivet: a hotplate
Tribble: a furry space bunny
Triffid: a bitchy yam

 Like   Comment   Share

Proposed clickbait titles to make people feel terrible

You're Doing Sleep Wrong and It's Killing Your Closest Friendships
Why Even Thinking Swears Will Damage Your Child's Emotional Growth
The Wrenching Truth behind Chocolate
5 Reasons You Should Ditch Soft Cheese (#3 Is a Shocker)
You've Been Breathing Wrong Your Entire Life
The Shocking Reason Your Dog Should Not Have an Internet Presence
Tell Us What Year You Were Born & We'll Tell You How You're Destroying America
Which Dog Breed Is Secretly Your Mother?
25 Reasons Your Anxiety Is Killing Your Pets

 Like   Comment   Share

Never Change, Gen X

I wanted to know how my generation had hurt the world
(but only a little),

So I did a quick search and found one lonely article
about my people:
"Gen X Ruined the World Too!"

And that pretty much sums up Gen X's lifelong quest for
validation.

 Like   Comment   Share

More terrible clickbait headlines to make you feel bad

Not Just a Crush: Your Obsession with Hot Celebs IS
Ruining Your Marriage
10 Reasons Houses Are Dangerous for Dogs
This Surprise Body Part Is Failing Right Now
Your Favorite Show Is Ruining Your Life—Here's Why
5 Crucial Memories Your Favorite Song Lyrics Have
Erased
3 Reasons Rejecting Toxic Friends Is Making YOU the
Toxic Friend
Think Positively or Risk Losing Everything

 Like   Comment   Share

Note to self 2

That is not Chapstick.
That is a glue stick.

 Like Comment Share

Life in Lockdown

Parentine

Mom.
MOM.

The small little voice
At the top of the stairs
Down the hall
Right next to my ear in the dim light of morning
On the other side of the shower curtain
Five seconds after bedtime

Mom. Mooooooooom.
What is it, sweetie?
I need someone to socialize me!

This tiny copy of me, insistent on our attention at all
times, because if his parents don't see him, how can he
exist?

Mom. Who was Henry XIII? Did he invent plums?
He invented divorce?
Oh. I like plums.

Why do people have children?
I asked the question once a long time ago, back when
people had blogs
I was thinking about it. I was making a list of pros and
cons, but having a child is not like buying a Nissan.
The pro and con approach doesn't work because it's not
about the quantifiable items: the gas mileage and the
turning radius.
It's not about features, like the airbags or the moonroof,
even.
It's something else.

Mom. MOM.
I do not like Frozen.
No? Why not, buddy?
Elsa's bad for the environment.

So I asked – I know why people don't have kids but why do people have kids?
And no one could give me a good answer.
They tried.
They gave me answers
But they were not real answers, not the answers, I was looking for
The answers I got were stories about the love they had for their own kids,
Photos of their babies and grandchildren
And nebulous, unasked-for predictions for my own future
Those were answers in a language I didn't speak.

Mom. MOM. We're camping out in the field tonight
There's a bobcat back there. I don't think that's a great idea.
You have to try new things, you know, Mom.

I don't have answers now, either.
Although my answer is in the air I breathe
Every day
Every minute
At night I sneak in to look at my answer when he sleeps
And I'm in the house with my answer
Doing remote school with my answer
I'm finding my answer things to do
And people to play safely with
And making my answer wear a mask
And providing *him* with answers

And waiting for a time when we can breathe again...
even if we're a little afraid to

Mom? Moooom? I want to kill the coronavirus.
I have great news about handwashing, buddy.
NOT LIKE THAT MOM

I take pictures, too.
I'll try not to offer them up if anybody asks why they
should have kids
I know that's not the answer they're looking for.

 Like　　　 Comment　　　 Share

Online learning

"Watch me do a crazy jump"
was NOT what I wanted to hear my kid say
during remote school

👍 Like   💬 Comment   ➦ Share

How hard can music be?

Every Monday I help my kid with music class
I think "he loves music, I love music, this will be easy."
And every Monday, there's a
breathing exercise,
a warm up,
two songs,
a dance
a craft
the identification of a classical instrument
and the deterioration of our familial bond.

 Like　　　 Comment　　　 Share

End of book being read in first grade: "That's why you should follow your heart. The end."
Tom: "TW, it's still class. Sit back down. Where are you going?"
TW: "I AM FOLLOWING MY HEART"

 Like   Comment   Share

Going into a store in person for the first time in seven months

It's wonderful!
Marvelous!
So many products!
No week of waiting!
No shipping charges!
I don't have to know those three numbers on the back of my credit card!

Is it possible this CVS
Is the most magical shop on the planet?

Almost quaint
I saw real paper money!

What if I want candy?
Or chips?
I can have them!
Oh look:
Pens!
Nail polish!

Music is playing!
People are here!
People who do not live with me!
I can see half their faces

But they're getting too close now
It's time to go home.

 Like   Comment   Share

Lockdown parenting

Them: "Someday you'll miss these days, Mama."
Me: "My kid has been talking nonstop since March 13."

Them: "Make memories! Dance like no one is watching!"
Me: "He does a lot of things like no one is watching."

Them, turning into motivational posters,
Peeling themselves from my social media,
Flapping around my room,
Trying to settle on my wall,
"Love. Laugh. Live.
You have to look through the rain to see the rainbow!
Aim for the moon and you'll land among the stars!"

Me: *gets matches*

 Like   Comment   Share

Acknowledgments

First, I need to start by thanking my husband Tom. He not only supports my writing, but he allows me to write about him, which is a big deal for such a private person. Thank you love, I couldn't have written this book without your quiet humor and all the material you give me.

I also want to thank T.W., who won't read this for a while, because he's only just starting to read. Buddy, you're a source of constant inspiration. Your joy and the way you see the world is a marvel to me.

I want to thank Karen Walsh, who came up with#WorldsOkayestMom. Thank you for letting me use it. It's honestly the only way I can describe my parenting now. Thank you also to Daniel Warren of Honja Photography, for your wonderful author pictures.

Thank you to everyone at Woodhall Press: Chris, Colin and especially David, who worked with me and put up with my late submissions for a full year. This is a book I never expected to publish, but your hard work made this happen. Thank you!

Lastly, thank you to all my Facebook friends. I make jokes on Facebook — you let me know when they work (and when they don't). So you were my writers' workshop for this book. Thank you for your input and your laughing reacts. I literally could not have written this without you.

Author bio

A.J. O'Connell joined social media back in the mid-'90s, when she barely had a real-life human adult identity for herself. Since her first cringy forays into chatrooms, she's been on AIM, Friendster, MySpace, blogged, tweeted, has been on the 'gram, and, obviously, Facebook. (She doesn't get TikTok, don't @ her.) She writes things in real life too. She's a freelance journalist and marketing writer, and her two novellas, Beware the Hawk and The Eagle & The Arrow, were published by VBP Press. A.J. lives in Connecticut with her family and entirely too many pets.